CW01645552

Liberties

For my family
and friends

'Order is never observed; it is disorder that attracts attention because it is awkward and intrusive.'

Eliphas Levi

Contents

Waltz

Hangover heavy
he sags into the chair

snarls answers to
questions they
haven't yet asked:

yes, no
yes, yes no

yes, no and
no comment

quite possibly
and
quite possibly
not.

Shoes

Now they're with the forensic team
the boy's shoes will tell them
more than he's been willing to.

His young hands too; swabbed with
sterile water and a maternal lightness
as the cotton tip alights on his palm

then strokes the back of his hand
to bring any trace of
the other boy back to life.

I wasn't always like this

What a noise she makes, what a need
for attention not even her constant calls
to the emergency services can relieve.

When they mention her previous
she laughs. I'm a walking crime wave
she says at the sudden recognition.

The young olds

Come on, come and do your dabs
but he rolls away his shoulders
fist fights the air and slurs another Special Brew curse.

Plasma beads the cut behind his ear
dried blood creates its own black stitches.

Chicken and rice, chicken and rice
he starts to sing
but they misunderstand.

They think he wants his rights.

He can’t speak

his own language
today, but he’s in a
familiar place where

nothing
feels like home

everything
feels like nothing

Are you alright?

A little while later he shakes his head no.

Blue love

The man who's done
twenty years has a
blur of blue love
on his knuckles and wants
to go straight and talks
and talks and falters
only when he recalls
his girlfriend going with
his two best friends;
he catches his breath
blinks back familiar tears
and tries to banish the
dissolute image
we can all picture now.

His salt water story falls
a sad slow rain
but he won't accept a tissue.

She has

She has a cough;
a Shirley Bassey
tobacco hack
and little else –

except the bags under
her eyes which droop
in pretty perfect
semi-circles on
sleepless sunken skin.

Untitled

He writes no comment
in the air with his finger
pokes and punctuates
each invisible syllable
to hold their questions at bay
for as long as he can.

A night out

Dip-dye hair
fun & fury
coke & whatevah
no I nevah

punched drunk
sobered up

hotel rooms
and interview suites

sleeves up:
red bruises
bloom blue.

Love that day

I

It's Valentine's Day
an old man
can't walk home
so they arrange a car
but before he leaves
he writes a note;
thanks someone
for coming to his cell
for talking to him
for listening to him
for treating him with dignity;
the young man
puts the gratitude
in his pocket and smiles:
whatever happens next
there was love
that day.

II

He'd done it twice the night before.
Woke her up (separate beds)
asked for more.
Third time lucky? No.

A cell in the Royal Academy

His cell in China is replicated
scaled down, bite-size
for London eyes

through the peephole:
Ai Wei Wei's in bed
his feet stick out

guards face him
they try to police his sleep

miniature cleaning products
lean against the wall

what's going to be
wiped away?

This is not a love thing

Scene one
Boy have you been a lucky girl
new in town and everybody's darling –
love, desire and a tender touch always
has the boys high for candy kisses
little miss. Beware the late night
luxury love, enjoy the good times for a day.

Scene two
Introducing a girl in a million
a young mistress, tamed and
trained with a luxury new apartment
and a wardrobe full of fun and games.
She's fresh and lovely, a cherry ripe
English rose. Fresh and green
she must be seen.

Scene three
Come on gentlemen, report now!
She's a genuine siren, talented
and in control. Urgent, be warned
your afternoon fun just got
censored. It's playtime with
visiting magistrates. Wonderland
is fantasy land now.

Scene four
So, a total transformation for
the country girl. Complete captivation
caged and reduced to tears. A taste of
no mercy, a broken sentence. Bow and
show repentance!

Scene five
Great, she's back in town
in pain. Feel the sensation
it's agony – friends, caring
friendly and understanding
a lifetime too late. Ouch.

Scene six
Demonstrate respect for the
pleasure princess. This is not
a love thing. She's heaven bound;
it's judgement day for all. Relax
enjoy the rest Venus.

It’s night already

November adds another winter minute
to this autumn afternoon; there’s nothing
in his pocket but the lighter he’s used on
his last cigarette and a photocopy map
to a hostel; the fluorescent pink swoop
of highlighter pen illuminates the way.

My letters now

Every letter asks for action
every letter starts with Yo!

Two inch kisses for a girl
coded hash tags for a friend.

Takes words without permission
breaks every language law.

A sonnet for nobody

What's up Ulysses? After a night in custody
he needs a KFC but it's all Prêt-a-Manger
round here, so wheels his moped across
pavements, hefts it past office workers
headed for mirrored offices where the sun
flashes one-eyed off the windows; the bike
he loves is dead-body-heavy so he stops at
a News Express for a packet of Haribo
still ten city miles from home he thinks
about the road ahead, and the beast
that is Brixton who lies in wait for a story
like his; a moped he can't ride. The police
have lost his helmet but warn he'll be back
if they catch him riding home without it.

Make way

for the one-legged man who gets carried in
like a battering ram. His outrage bursts
through the door before he does, police hands

keep him bowed; bald head and shirtless
curses, his camouflage trousers a nod
to a battle that's only just begun.

His wheelchair and belongings follow.

Who do you love

Who do you care about, the judge
asks the young person
who nods towards their mum
the judge
says of course, but tell me
who else? Their nan
they say, nan's don't judge.

He wears

He wears someone else's story;
a Leavers Class hoody: 2009
sixty names he's never met

wet from the rain they'll give him
a sweatshirt – overcast grey –
which he can keep, call his own.

There's a war on somewhere

He punch punishes the soldier he once was
left hooks his left cheek
splits an already fine line
from a shaving nick this morning
jabs a finger at his temple:
I'm not thick you know
but the shadows of his old sergeant
father, teacher still tell him that he is.

A cigarette and a Playstation

We sit next to a man with a potato pale face
thin with a hooked nose and blue blanket
that swamps him with colour.

He mimes a robbery; a hammer blow
shows empty pockets, pulls them out like rabbit ears.
The boy next to me is impressed

says he might try this next time. Bang.
Describes his future punch on a member
of the public with gunshot energy.

Says it won't be women. Only men.
It could be someone I know, I say.
He laughs. Even the pale man tells him

it's not a good idea. You'll get six for that.
The boy pretends he's on a Playstation
fakes a fag in his mouth – he's already there

in his future cell: tell me where
your friends live, I'll leave them alone
he says. They're everywhere, I say.

Not another night

He describes the space in his cell;
arms outstretched –
a fisherman recalling a catch.

Says he'll hit his head on the wall
to get himself anywhere
but here again tonight.

Shows off knuckles where a ladder of
rough stitches recount another time
his hand split apart in protest.

A young woman walks by, his leg
drives and up and down as she passes,
stops when she leaves.

He goes back
to dreading
tonight.

CCTV

a backlit patchwork
of screens that move
more than the people
on the vinyl mattresses do

who wait in their sleep
for solicitors, interviews
and decisions from the CPS.

The low ceilings
and lack of windows
make time in there
very hard to judge.

Prescription

He needs his methadone more than
he needs me, won't look up from
the table where he rests his head
and breathes a forceful rhythm;
are you asleep? But his feet are not
the feet of a sleeping man
they pump up and down
and say what he tries to hide
under his crumpled posture.

Blue hands

for when you kick off and the police race
to raid the box of blue gloves before
anything else and pull the deflated latex hands
out like tissues for tears to come and put
the gloves on like surgeons, in case, in case
and create one more layer away from you.

You'll never know

the muscles   required
to keep what   really
happened   inside
use your   right
to remain   silent
don't worry your   story
just wants the same   thing
as you do   release.

Everything hurts in here

I

Staples unbent from the Evening Standard
splinters of plastic cutlery drawn
across the skin, fork prongs that measle arms
t-shirts ripped into noose-long strips
bras and panties strangle too.

II

The old man with the walking stick
takes his time getting to the cell; he's frail
and cautious and treated with care
but when he's alone he'll snap his glasses
into spikes and knife-sharp shards
with no intention of hurting anyone but himself.

Can you get me a whip home bruv?

I ask the sergeant and
the sergeant says no.

She just needed to see you

No siren needed
for this nightdress
nine nine nine:

a broken mother
a shattered window.

Her robe is the colour of caramel
her wrists red from resisting;
but the bruise on her hand
blooms true.

Marvel

The blanket from his cell
flares like a cape as he
walks down the corridor;
a split-second superhero
who turns left into the
fingerprint room where
he sits and shivers
even though it's warm.

Who's going to believe it

What if the curtains did catch fire because of the TV?
What if the landlady did like having you living there?
What if you did get along with the people above you?
What if you really do have a Gainsborough on the wall?

Nice like this

Tears bring them running
they fall over themselves
to help, to listen, to reassure
but this just makes him angry;
he says his mother should
have been nice like this.

Says thank you miss
whoever helps him
but there's nothing
anyone can ever do.

Under here

The young woman won't come out
from under the blue blanket.
She's created a darkness
escaped the fluorescent hours;
made a place that can't be torn.

A child has gone.
A child has been taken.
She has to start again.
Curls herself into foetal sleep
says leave me alone, and they do.

In your own words

There is outrage when she hears the words:
nasty words she says, words
she can not hear again because they
sicken her. I am deeply spiritual she
insists until someone else agrees. In
an aria of pain and indignation she's
encouraged back into the room where
they hold her words, words taken down
in an embroidery of black biro.

An email re: the rapist rumours (which still persist)

You may have seen the posters requesting
information about these incidents.

They were traced to a film maker hoping
to benefit from the story.

He's been told his actions have helped to
increase the fear of crime locally and has

apologised. He's also confirmed that the
posters he put up only generated nine replies;

these were people who'd heard the rumour.
None claimed any first-hand knowledge.

When you get home

He looks through your letterbox
tests the door, rings the bell:

is anyone there
is anyone there

but there isn't so he lets
the house swallow him.

CCTV continues the day outside:
a runner walks by
school children pass in an energetic knot

the house hides
what he's doing
what he's choosing

until he leaves
shape-shifts into
someone no one notices
past the dustman lifting up
the rubbish
black balloons of waste
today is garbage day –

and when you get home
all the good things will be gone.

Wait a minute

The automatic door startles at
everything; its mechanics hush
an already silent waiting room.

Everyone who crosses the
threshold is the lawyer
who'll be here in a minute

but it's a mum with a pram
and a phone to her ear
whose son's been nicked

for riding on the pavement
but will get charged for
something else; it's the lady

with the mud on her legs who
wants you to know she helped
the old man get his dog back.

A bus exhales. Internal doors
slam. A plastic triangle guards
a spill that's already dry. Chairs

are locked in a row; a mesh
of Met-blue metal that make
waiting here unforgiving.

There's a patch of false
sunlight worn clean by
nervous feet on the floor

A lady waits with a letter
that says she was depressed;
shows it to everyone, it's here

in black and white. She blots
her tears with a tissue from
the sergeant. Outside smokers

pull hard on their cigarettes
smoke finds its way in
hovers like weather above her.

The ivy on Wormwood Scrubs

It's leafless here; winter bare
even in summer. Lifeless ivy
varicose veins on the wall
chart where the suckers hold on.

Someone from the council has
taken a knife to it.

He’s Bad

He’s bad
he’s good
he’s misunderstood

Empty cells

He grabs a few more minutes of sleep under the
darkness of his hood while he waits on the bench
to be charged with stealing food.

Says he can't buy food let alone pay the fine
the sergeant nods, gives him a leaflet for support
microwaves an extra meal before he leaves.

The everyday, every day

He would like to appear a reasonable man.
He has a daily routine.
He wakes up. He has a coffee.
He has a cigarette and reads the papers.
He goes to the corner shop
and buys a bottle of coke. His afternoons
are spent watching the television.

At night
he goes to bed.

I'm not a person who
kicks the ladies, he says
and part of him believes it.

Appropriate

Anyway, has he eaten?
Yes.
Sausage and potato –
a microwaved
ready meal
in cardboard
he makes a face
reveals the years of cigarettes
filtered by his teeth.

And then he remembers

someone gave him
curried goat
rice and peas once

his face lights up
clouds over
when he can't remember
who it was.

Young girl alone

How old do you think she is?
Her nails are perfect. Red painted
puddles. Pink polish on her toes.
But there's too youthful a roundness
to her face, adolescent tilt to her voice.
Tears and tissues chart a lonely story
that started a long way away.

We have to leave her soon:
everyone will have done their job
not even the interpreter can stay.

News to me

Here's the truth: it's a
story within a story
details without denial
a long and winding road
of exaggerated explanation
that becomes hard to follow.

Have some hot sweet tea.

But this elicits more tales
of crack cocaine and uncles
who weren't uncles.
your concentration
wanders; hasn't he got
luxuriant hair for
someone so troubled?

Lines

The girl says she's been bruised

makes an instant protest poster
pages from a notebook that say

they assault 17 year olds
exclamation mark
exclamation mark
exclamation mark.

Sticks it where she can

makes two more biro protests
before she decides to vocalise
her outrage to anyone who will listen.

But the people in the queue have
problems of their own

a woman objects
says she hasn't come here
to listen to things like this.

Recall

He can only remember the arrest.
He was in a market place.
Fruit and veg.
Out-of-date
biscuits and cakes
going cheap.

A dog was barking.
It was busy.
The police came up
wanted him
to go with them.

He keeps asking:

what if I've done
what I did
what will
happen to me?

Overdue

A man from Belarus has been asked to leave
the library; they say he can't come in again
but this is where he goes to use the computers
to email his family in Belarus. He's upset.

Gulps the air like a distressed child
says he feels persecuted. Shouts and shouts
until he draws the authorities towards him.
Maybe he could try another internet source?

But today is Tuesday. The day he couldn't
take it anymore. Everything has led to this day;
the library, the computer, whatever began
a lifetime ago was always due soon.

Every Jonah

sits in a cell the size of

a small whale:

tiles and a toilet

sometimes

three days, two nights

before they hand back

the ten pound note

and cigarette for over the ear.

When you leave

you'll heave your bag

out of the mouth of this

slow moving beast

stand on the pavement

and for a moment

forget which way is home.

Fifteen cages

the perfume of
too many dogs.
Notes of distress
resignation and
a scent of worse.

A dark woollen coat;
loose pet hairs that
punctuate a story
about to be told.

Heatwave

Her voice rounds the corner before she does
harpy sharps keep the boy behind her small
blame scorches the heat
her accusations slap
head down he carries a backpack like a pair of old wings
fused and folded for another time.

A refuge

Long hair and nicotine hands
mark the time since he cared.

His mood is derelict; his clothes
a ragged flag for a country
that's someone else's now

his posture surrenders too;
hunched and haunted he's
too big for this narrow bench.

Depression helps, he says
he sleeps well even here.

Wormwood Scrubs

A burnt out van
a curve of handbrake turns
carved into the grass:

scribbles of upholstery springs
a passenger seat skeleton

contact numbers ghost the side
the word plumber
a shadow now

tools in the back are
ruddy: tawny chisels
auburn bolts

an orphaned saw blade

something that looks like
a monkey's head: hollow eyes
and a wide smile that laughs
it was once of use too.

If you're asking me

She's not doing anything now.
She's smoking dope.

She's not materialistic.
She's got problems of her own.

Tenderloin

San Francisco

Ashen skin; a
drug Pompeii

everyone talks to
no one

itchy lunch lines:
daylight dread

crack creates
a democracy:

but little
tender here.

The H26

From Hatton Cross to Sparrow Farm
Heathrow waves between the houses:
runway, radar, chain link fence
a flash of passenger plane that
takes you anywhere but here.

See the person not the prisoner

Mums get ready;
bring a pound
for the lockers –
they don't have change.
Stand like a scarecrow
for the pat, pat, pat
of mistrust
listen for the keys
behind the door;
set your smile to reassure.

Bird

The trapped sun
warms the bricks
browns the lilac

nature exploits
the cracks
in the concrete

there's a gap
a no-man's-land
between the bars.

Bracken creeps
towards it but
there's nowhere

for it to go
but back into
the overlooked.

The net above
makes the garden
another cage

a blackbird
darts by
at ankle height

a feather caught
shudders its
downy fingers

a lilac tree
makes it
through the net;

other plants
bow their
heads instead.

More from the garden

Small plants stay small
in the rivalry for a sun
you can't rely on.

Everything asserts itself here
stray seeds dropped by a bird:
rape, two plants' worth.

But the sound of the rain
on the leaves isn't applause.

Never Met

This trouble maker
gang member

scum

is willing to answer any question
but can't because of the rat-a-tat-tat
of his every reply; words hostage
to a stammer that's so severe
everyone else is lost for words.

Lying

They wait while she sleeps
snores a steady objection
to every request; not even
her name can find her.

She lies under the blankets
hides under the layers:
did she do what she did
or did she do what she did

because someone did it
to her? No one's allowed
to touch but they lift
the covers anyway –

she wears an evening gown.
Chanel. The sequins throw back
the light, wink even in this
dim little room.

Document this

A sheath of legal documents
held up like a paper hand
says back off, keep away
but he's broken the order:

there's no chance of
no comment
incriminates himself
with unspent fury

can't even stop
when his lawyer drags
a finger across his
throat to remind him.

He has nothing

In spite of
his young years alone
he smiles

in spite of
his mum's addiction
he's warm

in spite of
a fingerprint found
he laughs

in spite of
everything we know –
he has

nothing
to worry
about.

Halloween

Sad and sorry
The Joker
rings
his mum.

A witch in
deliberate
tatters
leans

across the counter
to hear
her
charge.

Burglar Bill
laughs –
they've
taken his

photo
but forgot to
wipe off
his mask.

Two blue lights

In the car they talk about a colleague
someone not wanted on their team;
CID will have them
they'll have anyone.

The Holloway Road is busy
so they drive a parallel universe
north past a shuttered police station
closed because of the cuts.

The radio on the dashboard
stutters a request they ignore.

One drives while the other studies
a car on YouTube as it shunts
another car in its attempt to park.
He laughs at his phone and you hear
the word idiot somewhere in his delight.

An undercover car barrels towards them;
two blue lights sashay side-to-side
flashes them out of its way.

Bone china shadows

Sweep the teacups from the table
give the painted birdies flight –
only hearts can break
these china platters.

            That's a thousand pounds
he says and
            I'm calling the police.

Shards hurt less
than lack of
interest.

The past of Rita and Christina

Ask him if the sky is blue and he'll
tell you instead about Rita and Christina
and the crooked lawyer, in a poetry of
broken Italian the interpreter says
it is important not to correct.
The more he says, the more he has to say;
brings a sudden thunder
to this small sealed room
strikes himself again and again
bangs a book on the table
bellows until the policeman with
the coiled calm, and hands that ask
for pianissimo, tries to reach him
past the past of Rita and Christina.

Untitled

A small hard smile
where laughter
marries fury.

You don't believe him
do you.

Cash fans

The laptop opens like a treasure chest
reveals a boy holding a cash sandwich
his face obscured by a pile of money
layered between two slices of white bread.

Someone else anchors folded twenties
to their head with a cap, he's a cash clown
with cash hair, looks into the camera like
he's helped himself to Mona Lisa's smile.

Other boys mimic senoritas, wave fans
of cash on the doorstep. Multi-coloured fans;
blue, red, green, all in currency order
fifties in tidy circles of pink and brown.

The proactive unit

Mug shot squares printed fast on cheap paper
curl away from the wall –
a gang held apart by drawing pins.

Each boy is his own country now:

the one with the seaweed fringe lifts his face
to the camera, another sits like he's waiting for a bus
his shirt the same grey as the hood
on the boy who sits low in the frame.

A fourth boy narrows his eyes; forehead rippled
beyond its years. The boy next-door surprises
with the shadow of a moustache
stars of acne on his young face.

The boy with the everyday name triggers
a recognition beyond the photo –
an early morning shadow in the road.

But it's the one with the broken nose
that stops you. Makes you think of his
mother: a Hollister t-shirt, once white
is now washing-machine grey.

He takes

liberties
and iPhones
misplaces loyalty
but creates family from friends
when there's no one at home
to notice he's not.

Can you imagine what the other person feels like?

But he can only see
the pain he's caused
his mother who sits
beside him
still shaking her head
in disbelief.

May day

On the first day of spring
four boys make the most
of the acoustics of their cells
they call to each other;
voices bounce off
wash-down walls
names roam with liberty.

No one will eat here, no one
will drink here: they wait
until they get out.

Fingerprints get taken.
Press and roll.
Press and roll.
Each print a swirl of fine black
lines, a topographic map
of another world. When it gets late
they call again:

if you don'tget out tonight
we'll take care of things.

The bond is strong
it's a lot like love.

Jack-in-the-box

A *National Enquirer*
face-down on the pavement

carrier bags pillows against a doorstep

a sleeping shape under
someone else's eiderdown
other people's coats;

a textile pupa that doesn't move

until

a blanket slips
pools at his feet

then he's up
awake
accusing everyone.

Misled

He's in for a scam and a laugh
never been to school so can't
even pass the time reading;

would he like a magazine
with pictures? No one here for
you now for all your brudders

and tisters. Tears as he hangs
his head; a fag would be good
his manners are impeccable

and the sergeant knows he's
vulnerable; younger than
his thirty years and can't

cope, so takes him out for
some car park daylight
and a cigarette in handcuffs

which won't stop him having
two. The sergeant's decent
but the shift will change soon.

He's coaxed into something to
eat, sweet and sour chicken
but it turns out to it be tuna bake.

Believe me

A small room
an open door.
A stage for one
voice: he says
who can speak
and who can't
so shut it. Says his
world is coming
to collect a debt
from this one:
nods to everyone
outside, runs a
finger across his
throat, paints a
picture of a fury
not yet spent.

Teumessian fox

Laelaps says
you do not have to say anything

and he doesn't
his mouth tightens so
nothing can escape

a couple of rusty coffee spills
on a clean white shirt
hair the colour of red brick
feet in custody issue shoes:
a tell-tale twitch of the leg

only when they say
they have his DNA.

The clockwise chase on the M25
should have lasted an eternity.

Release

The boy's mother arrives
frightened and furious

unable to speak she raises
her hand to his head and

brings it down to stroke
the side of his face instead.

Bambi

The boy who laughs at nothing
puts the DVD under his coat –
he'll watch the cartoon later.

A security guard puts a hand on his shoulder:

the boy is miles from home (10)
miles from being a boy (29).

Fly

The paper-fine plastic
of the disposable cup
is bone china sheer.

The fly trapped under it
makes a charcoal smudge
that climbs the ribbed wall

like it's a ladder to somewhere.
The buzz and click of
captivity is amplified by

the shape of the cup and
the silence in the cell.
The boy on the bed has

never been in a place
like this before; doesn't know
who he is waiting for.

When the metal door opens
it creates a breath that tips
the cup, releases the fly.

The Jack o'Lantern man

Missing front teeth
a bald head
and an archive of scars
from past and future fights.

He's excitable, drunk;
the morning after is
still the night before

he lists his prisons like poetry:

Pentonville
Wormwood Scrubs
Wandsworth.

says he's so coarse, so crude
even calls himself a cunt.

The visitor

He lets you in.

His pony tail's a dark coil whose length tallies
with the years he's lived in the house.
The house where the table wobbles
even though he's a builder, where the
steel pots clatter on the cooker
boiling with the unknown. There's
more than one tall fridge here:
one, two, three. A domestic forest.

When he can't find the words he gestures:
two fingers jab at his neck
teeth, teeth he says, pulls up a trouser leg
mimes a knife strapped to his ankle;
charades to guess the old country.

You steal glances:
What's out the back?
What's under the tarpaulin?
You look for an afternoon drama
when there isn't one.

Twenty four

Juliet plays with a dog
tickles it and talks about her family;
Juliet's got eye-liner-eyes
and a roller-coaster pony tail;

her boyfriend walks through the door
thin arms tattooed with the relief he found
at the end of a plastic fork last night.

Bewildered, pale, he looks like someone
from a black and white film
who finds himself back in
Juliet's technicolour world.

Carina, Carina, Carina

Spread-eagled shirts, shoes, a lone suitcase;
spent missiles that tell tales on the night before
she yells from an open window (two floors up)
once Juliet to the man who sways below
on the patch of grass in front of the flats
who's ignoring the glances of passers-by
to chant his worn out words, give him another
chance, please Carina please, the three syllables
in her name the loveliest thing about her.

White Lightning was popular back then

A November night. A moon like a fingernail clipping.
A man staggers from a day on White Lightning

a slack-stringed-marionette who can defy gravity
until he walks in front of a moving car and then silence

a muffled cry from the driver; pleads and pleases
a desperate bargain with the sky until the man rises

up on his feet, back from the dead, White Lightning
giving both of them another chance.

Nothing Hill

We step back to make way for
the large man cradling
a collection of vinyls to his chest.

We step back again to give
the record shop assistant
the chance to catch him.

Neighbours listen

An open window sucks his voice
into the warm night air.

A man's dog-bark delivery
petty accusations broadcast
with practiced fury. It's her fault

and always will be
but it's her silence we listen to.

Go home Margaret

Margaret raises her voice in the market
calls the stall holder who wears fake flowers
in her hair; a prostitute
her children; crack addicts.

She's shouting with such vigour
she takes a seat outside a café
to support her senescent frame

I'm buying potatoes and carrots
telling the stall holder I recognise
Margaret from the days she'd ring
Ron's doorbell.

Go home Margaret, the stall holder says
every now and then
but Margaret's happy where she is.

Flowers from a supermarket in March

On a path by a prison
a bunch of brittle brown roses
still hold their shape in April.

Written in biro
paled by the rain
notes pinned to the cellophane say:

to Nick you-silly-little-shit from your
ugly old mother-in-law, and to Daddy
love Katy.

Joy

The grass ploughed and ripped
from the mud
maps a night of illicit handbrake turns
accelerated joy.

A Kwik-Fit receipt
flaps on the ground
the car doors spread themselves
with the come on
of a game show prize.

Dedication

There's a tree over there, she says
that the Queen planted sixty years ago
but you wouldn't know it
because someone's nicked the plaque.

Microsoft

The boy learns Microsoft to keep
his future books looking straight.

The boy learns to listen, points out
defensive gestures like crossing your arms.

The boy learns to ask open questions:
his girlfriend tells him everything now.

All night for nothing

Bright red Converse shoes match
the checked shirt of this young meteor
incandescent from the friction of
being kept all night for nothing;
she has a case for fury –
as she's released into the room
her head high
hair a bedhead of flame
her mood veers north
falls south

Out of season

A young Roma girl
without shoes
in a town out of season
begs at a car window.

The driver aims a gun
of pointed finger and
erect thumb and laughs
as he shoots her.

One way to escape

Pentonville October 2016

The acoustics of locked doors
and little windows
an echo of trainers on
worn-out lino

a blast of bass from voices
in a canteen unseen

too many men:
words on signs that warn
do not, do not, do not

but twenty-six people
find a moment from every bad sentence
they've ever told themselves

a restitution, a restoration

as they listen to someone else's story
and understand
this could be a moment of liberty.